The
Salmon

Published by Raintree Steck-Vaughn Publishers, an imprint of Steck-Vaughn Company.

Acknowledgments
Project Editor: Helene Resky
Design Manager: Joyce Spicer
Consulting Editor: Kim Merlino
Consultant: Michael Chinery
Illustrated by Colin Newman
Designed by Ian Winton and Steve Prosser
Electronic Cover Production: Alan Klemp
Additional Electronic Production: Bo McKinney and Scott Melcer
Photography credits on page 32

Planned and produced by The Creative Publishing Company

Library of Congress Cataloging-in-Publication Data
    Crewe, Sabrina
    The salmon / Sabrina Crewe
       p.   cm. — (Life cycles)
    Includes index.
    Summary: Describes the habitat, eating habits, and life cycle of the sockeye salmon.
    ISBN 0-8172-4371-2 (hardcover). — ISBN 0-8172-6234-2 (pbk.)
    1. Salmon — Juvenile literature.   2. Sockeye salmon — Juvenile literature.   3. Salmon — Life cycles — Juvenile literature.   4. Sockeye salmon — Life cycles — Juvenile literature.
[1. Sockeye salmon 2. Salmon.]   I. Title.   II. Series: Crewe, Sabrina. Life cycles.
QL638.S2C835   1997
597'.55 — dc20   96-4834
                                          CIP   AC

   3 4 5 6 7 8 9 0 LB 00 99 98
Printed and bound in the United States of America.

Words explained in the glossary appear in **bold** the first time they are used in the text.

LIFE CYCLES

The
Salmon

Sabrina Crewe

RSVP

**RAINTREE
STECK-VAUGHN**
PUBLISHERS
The Steck-Vaughn Company

Austin, Texas

The salmon has hidden her eggs.

The salmon has laid her eggs on the bottom of the river. She has covered the eggs with **gravel**, which helps keep them hidden. Inside the eggs, salmon **embryos** are growing.

Soon the mother salmon will drift away. The baby salmon will look after themselves when they **hatch**.

The salmon is hatching.

After eight weeks, the salmon embryo
breaks the egg with its tail. The embryo
is coming out. Now it is called a **larva**.

The larva feeds on its yolk.

The **yolk** of the egg is still attached to the larva. This will be its only food for the next few weeks. The larva stays hidden in the gravel.

The salmon has left the nest.

The salmon is several weeks old. It has become a young fish. The salmon eats tiny animals in the river, such as water fleas and insect larvae.

The salmon is eating fish.

Now the salmon is nearly one year old.
It has started to to hunt small fish. It
catches **minnows** in its sharp teeth.

The salmon are migrating.

The salmon is two years old. It has grown much larger. The dark spots on its body have disappeared. The salmon is ready to **migrate**.

The salmon are leaving the river where they were born. They are migrating to the ocean.

The salmon have reached the ocean.

The salmon have traveled hundreds of miles. Other groups of salmon have arrived in the ocean at the same time. They have come from many different rivers.

The salmon find plenty to eat in their new home. They live on **shrimp** and small fish, such as **anchovies**. The salmon grow quickly in the ocean.

Salmon travel in groups.

As they move around the ocean, salmon stay together in groups called schools. A big school will frighten away small enemies. It will also protect the salmon when larger fish attack.

After three years in the ocean, the salmon are fully grown. They migrate back to the river where they were born. They know their own river by the smell of the water.

The salmon leap up a waterfall!

The salmon have reached their river. When they come to a waterfall, the salmon jump high out of the water to reach the top.

The salmon meet other dangers on their
journey. There are sharp rocks along the
way. Bears often wait to catch salmon
as they migrate.

The salmon have changed color.

The salmon spend many weeks traveling
up the river. As they swim, they start to
look different.

The sides and back of the salmon become
bright red. The tops of their heads turn green.
The male salmon grow hooked jaws.

The salmon have found their old home.

After many weeks, the salmon reach the
river where they hatched. The salmon
are very tired and thin. They have had
no food on their journey.

The salmon are fighting.

The male salmon are **competing** for a
female salmon. The salmon that wins
the fight will **fertilize** the female's eggs.

The female salmon is digging a nest.

The salmon uses her tail to make a
hole in the gravel on the bottom of
the river. She is making a safe place
to lay her eggs.

The salmon swim side by side.

The male and female salmon are over the nest. The female salmon lets out her eggs. The male lets out his **sperm** over the eggs. When an egg and sperm join, a new salmon can grow.

The salmon dies after it has spawned.

The salmon are worn out by their long migration. They die after **spawning**.

Salmon need clean water.

Salmon are in danger because the rivers where they live have become **polluted**. Dams across rivers may stop salmon from returning to their streams. People can help by keeping rivers clean and not catching too many salmon for food.

Parts of a Salmon

Salmon are fish. Fish are animals with **backbones** that live and breathe in water. Most fish are covered in **scales**. Fish live in streams, rivers, ponds, lakes, and oceans.

2nd dorsal fin
Used for balance

Tail fin
Used to push the fish through water

Anal fin
Used for balance

Pelvic fins
Used for balance

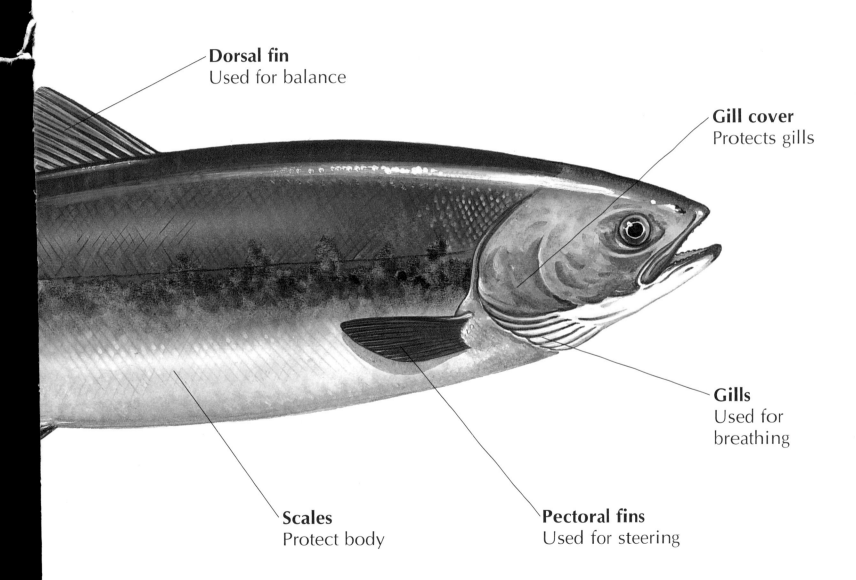

Dorsal fin
Used for balance

Gill cover
Protects gills

Gills
Used for
breathing

Scales
Protect body

Pectoral fins
Used for steering

Other Fish

The salmon in this book is a sockeye salmon. Here are some other types of salmon and different kinds of fish.

Humpback salmon

Chinook salmon

Goosefish

Pacific snake eel

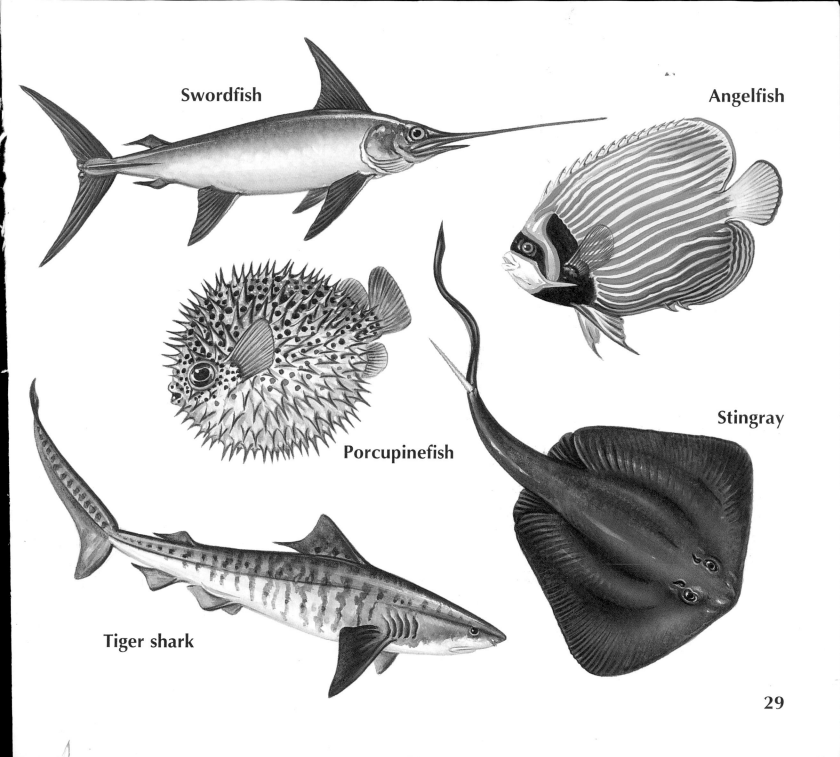

Swordfish

Angelfish

Porcupinefish

Stingray

Tiger shark

Where the Sockeye Salmon Lives

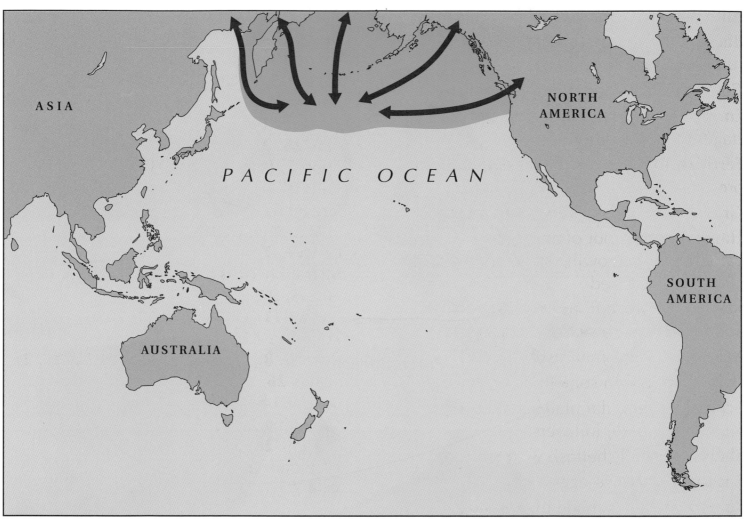

ASIA

NORTH
AMERICA

PACIFIC OCEAN

SOUTH
AMERICA

AUSTRALIA

 Areas where the sockeye
salmon lives

 Migratory routes of
the sockeye salmon

Glossary

Anchovy A type of small fish

Backbone The row of small bones running down an animal's back

Compete To try and win something

Embryo An animal in the first growing stages before it is born

Fertilize To make a female's eggs able to produce babies

Gravel A mixture of very small rocks

Hatch To come out of an egg

Larva The first growing stage of an animal after it has hatched

Migrate To move from one place to another when the seasons change

Minnow A very small fish

Pollute To poison something or make it dirty

Scales The thin, flat plates that cover an animal's body in layers

Shrimp A small shellfish with ten legs

Spawn To produce eggs

Sperm The seeds made by a male to fertilize a female's eggs

Yolk The part of an egg that provides food to the embryo and larva

Index